PEACE IN DURESS

Also by Janet Rogers

BOOKS

Splitting the Heart

Unearthed

Red Erotic

ALBUMS

Firewater

Got Your Back

6 Directions

PEACE IN DURESS

JANET ROGERS

Talonbooks

Talonbooks
278 East First Avenue, Vancouver, British Columbia, Canada V5T 1A6
www.talonbooks.com

First printing: 2014

Typeset in Janson
Printed and bound in Canada on 100% post-consumer recycled paper

On the cover: Shelley Niro, *Flying Woman 2*, 1993

Talonbooks gratefully acknowledges the financial support of the Canada Council for the Arts, the Government of Canada through the Canada Book Fund, and the Province of British Columbia through the British Columbia Arts Council and the Book Publishing Tax Credit.

Library and Archives Canada Cataloguing in Publication

Rogers, Janet Marie, 1963–, author
        Peace in duress / Janet Rogers.

Poems.
ISBN 978-0-88922-911-2 (pbk.)

        I. Title.

PS8585.O395158P43 2014   C811'.6   C2014-903252-8

I am a strong believer in the artist's role as witness and recorder of history. The poems in this collection invite the reader to take time and consider their own place in each poem. With each rally, march, and protest, with each petition, blockade, and occupation, we are given the opportunity to learn about ourselves when we ask the question, "How far am I willing to go for my convictions?"

I take seriously the responsibilities of being a writer and at the same time revel in the joy of creative words. I am grateful for female warriors, I am grateful for women artists everywhere who continue to push their work to the fore, I am grateful for the Salish People on whose territory I am allowed to be a visitor. Without the efforts and energies of these brave people, I would not know the great pleasure, enjoy the freedom, and have the ability to fulfill my purpose as a writer and performance poet.

My greatest wish is to inspire others, provide healing, and metaphorically march together with these poem offerings. I send a heartfelt thank-you to all the true activists, artists, and grassroots community organizers who dedicate themselves to the protection of our lands and our waters. The artist's voice is an essential and necessary part of resistance culture. May it always be heard and take its rightful place in our collective histories.

Janet Rogers
Victoria, August 2014

Contents

1. Land

3   Lekwungen Land

10 Body Language

12 Like a Lion

13 Three-Day Road

17 Forty Dayz

19 Love Is a Long Moan

22 Stroking the Serpent

26 I Was There

29 They Leave Their Names All over the Place

2. Culture

33 Forever

36 Here's the Deal

37 Five O'Clock

38 Hotel Reality

42 Birds Falling

44 The Celebrity of Famous

48 The Sexual Revolution Will Be Televised

51 Authent®ick

53 Red-Black

55 Witness

58 We Are Swimming

     Sky Woman Falling (a POV blog)

59   Part 1

61   Part 2

62   Part 3

63 Love and Protection

3. Poetry

69   3rd Stone from the Sun

71   Used to Be (Home)

73   We Are

76   Reject, Rejection, Accepted

79   He Ain't Comin' Back

81   Sap

82   Bearskin

84   Hang It on a Hook

87   Awake Awake

89   Surprise Me

92   Alotta Hullabaloo

94   A State of Mine

4. Politics

99   Louder than Ever

100   Move a Mountain (Walk a Mile in Her Shoes)

103   Eleven, Eleven

105   Who's Your Daddy

107   Acts of Emancipation

110   Giving a Shit

114   Is It Easier to Move from Indian to Acculturated
Eurocentric Assimilated Brown Skin?
Or the Other Way Around?

1

LAND

Lekwungen Land

The city is a midden
with layers of collective truth
ascending from 150 feet down

We are the fingertips
of the far-left arm
touching the liquid connector
holding the larger land mass together
Lekwungen land
where woven blankets are laid
across graves as a way
to say we honour those
who sleep beneath us
their song of welcome, victory, and journey
resonates faintly on ancient beaches
reaches our hearts

The mayor says
"Victoria tries so hard to be cool"
it's true
but cool on our own terms
we've never borrowed from
Big Sister Van-city
glossy steel-and-glass style
those shiny outfits would never fit us
never had need to copy
our southern cousin
Seattle, our shores
still accessible whatever
the consequence

Victoria
I like to think
was born to handsome parents
and abandoned awhile, surviving
a few seasons, living independently
learning a few things

an orphan adopting
other orphans
until finally
the family it wished for
was formed

Surely the best
definition of the city
sits outside the confines of 150
incorporation is a marriage
reciting vows in business language
between territory and people
and you can't marry the bride
without proposing to the whole
of her clan
without honouring
well at least recognizing
the relationships in all
their delicate dynamics
before congratulations are
sent

We've played the defensive
for more than a century
shaping and naming
the babies by what
we are not
let's be more
than the country's   .
superficial identity
of hockey, beer, and coffee
brewed by you-know-who

We are standing
on bones
we drink
from oceans

ill-named and renamed
yet it all stays the same
eighteen hundred and sixty-two when it became
paper-legal, a place existing
on a map, the map tucked away
as a file, finding a soul as a city
breathing life into the union
by human means

Sculptural landmarks
put in place, trace values
create one more layer
cultural excavation
within the city
atop Lekwungen land

Poetry and legalese
coexisting on home and native land
the city, the mystery
carries questions, digging in history
for answers to bring forward

It is difficult
to mark the years
as infant then adolescent
not knowing the exact
lifespan
of a city still growing
not knowing the beginning
before the naming and claiming
in Her Majesty's honour
celebration by incorporation connecting
borders crossing people's
homelands

Important councils
debate beauty, import labour
deliberate culture, ruminate history

As her children we learn
never to judge the worth
by one's outer beauty
although we know
we are gorgeous
and would not qualify for
any pageant due to
exceeding the aesthetic

Our greatest asset
is memory
the ships, the battle
the blankets, the blood
the people

That painter woman, her house
hotels replacing big houses

Allow me to step outside
the timelessness of this tribute
to put the Queen on Google Maps
where her sceptre extends out
like spokes
towards Esquimalt, Royal Oak
Saanich, View Royal, and others
she holds them up
sending citizens out from centre
inhabiting pockets of a city still
growing in population
follow her roads and we find
people, not contracts
land, not real estate
culture, not tourism

We review archival evidence
the before and after
value systems shifting

replacing simple simplicity
the silent skeletons
are finally having their say

Victoria, City of Gardens
with seeds blown in
from every direction
taking root among the indigenous
resulting in rich varieties
and cross-pollinations
the plump, happy-faced poppies
delicate, shy pansies
brother–sister seeds
that grow, despite the odds
from concrete cracks
surviving on thimbles of water
holding ground in bully gusts

The questions get harder
do we vote for more
lenient building bans
or take the keys to the city
from around our necks
to open doors
leading to wider highways
and faster transit

What about that mainland bridge?
this remains a dream
for the time being
future governments
can visit that museum of
possibilities

In this place
there is no need to abuse
the word "miracle"

misunderstand or exploit it
the constant sparkle
upon the water
and salmon sunsets define it
however her mysteries
remain thick
and those who protect
her beauty secrets
work harder with less
the salt-cleansed air
blesses us daily
as well as the fog
and constant June clouds

Here, the light is too
bright to be colour-blind
why ignore the rainbow
growing and changing
in shades like the aurora borealis
pushing one colour forward
pulling another back
constantly transforming
never stagnating
but celebrating
change

Today this occasion
may be too inadequate to
hold up the whole of history in one place
but sufficient enough
to make a marker in time
to witness what no living human
today can say
they've experienced from the start

In human years, 150 is a long time
in human years, 150 is a blip

So we take our place as collective witness
to tell the next generation
that 150 is both
long and short
for one day, when we are forced
from here
shaken or flooded or sunken back home
Lekwungen Land will sigh and say

"Take your stuff and things
leave me with my simple beauty
the same beauty that lured you here
in the first place."

Body Language

Circles
Earth dirt
Lines and colour
As above so below
Infinity and infinity
Salt-water body symbols
Language answers bold thought
Ask

Pungent imprints
Hard footprint paint
Rock talk resolutions
Human conditions
Measured in cause and effect
Tactics lacking natural elements
Compassionate relations
Forgetfulness will not come
Bolt

Prime numbers
Lined up and ready
Science and romance
Versus chemical warfare
Malevolent reactions
Unkind and likely
Placed in the middle
While mommy and daddy fight
Freeze

Star beings
Ready and watching
Scratching wounds
Touching reality
Do you believe?
Believe

Our bodies achieve
Beauty when spirit
Leaves, when flesh returns
To earth and we begin
To live again under the sun
Rumble and giggle
Sink and let go

Like a Lion

She
blew in
bringing her entire family
rain storm hail sisters
concentrated clouds fused to make grey
sky ceilings screaming under pressure
underground creatures feeling the shift
knowing on this day to take cover and remain

She
brings
new ways to think
we visit old friends in dreams
push memories to and fro
tornado warnings can't protect
or prevent what's coming
like emotional forecasts
we can never be ready
taste the doom in the air
like ice and electricity
change rustles the weakest
limbs clinging to forces
stronger than themselves

She
is exciting and threatening
this shift takes us
away from places of comfort
we build our reality inside stillness
but she is here to shake us
break us up so finding each other
becomes our purpose
find us

Three-Day Road

dirt doesn't want to stay down
welcome winds whip, nothing
is put back in place
dust storms and rain clouds
Halloween goblins appear
peeling earth sounds like lost love
left on horizons, behind, forgotten
wide open air, long sad stretches, sky
reaches down tenderly kisses earth
leaving rearranged landscape

no one travels roads
where birds are left hovering, not moving backward or
forward
just struggling against wind
sacrificial plastic bags plant themselves like flags
and wave their monochrome confessions
to anyone who cares to listen
evidence of man and nature. whatever

ice water now the temperature of tea sustains
until the next rez stop, re stop, restart
life elevated in Utah, gawd hours honoured in Arizona
tumble weeds and raw earth, looks like open battle wounds
gorges burnt earth sage brush holy land hot souls
long roads ash-fault
bill-borders built on the backs of black hispanics
descent warnings foreshadowing rocks falling
sun blocked bright rays make way for end-of-day rain
don't drink the poison, don't you dare sigh with boredom
hot winds die pulling down cloud poetry
faces, places, displaces, wide-open Red
horses of courses

this land is my favourite song that skips at my favourite part
that floats like boats from another land
rough ride, perilous endless packing experience

13

conquered with confidence we are promised
ice cream for goodness (sakes)
parcels of land expand in price buy a ticket, win a farm,
the canyons aren't kidding, the bluffs aren't bluffing
the towns aren't turning, don't give it a second thought

man's attempt at wit in creative critter names
Devil's Canyon, Eagle Ridge, Rattlesnake Lake
Fox Tail Trail, Horseshoe Pass, Billy Goat Harbour
Buffalo Landing, Prairie Fox Foothill
Raven's Ridge, Sleeping Giant Mountain

dried-up underwater world spitting back time
elevations challenge, motivations question
blocked hearts connect and autumn comes fast
forward forth a home for the free a home for the brave

broken barriers land borders
unbelievable scenarios that put people in their place
traced back to somewhere fake
where the idea of original is absolutely lost
but tell it like legends cobbled from inaccuracies
nationalism is a blank buffet feeding the starving
it's okay to forget who we are for a while
not forever   never forever

did I die? am I dreaming? I am drunk
I've never seen the world look so beautiful
the political is ironic all the talk dismisses this
this is where food comes from
this is where the moon lives too
the light makes love to the land every day
we stay here and play in this, all of this is home

suicidal plastic bags, frozen poses of roadkill critters
rivers, where women's bodies are littered
so many to make the two synonymous, Green River
this is a-merry-merry-merry-ca of visitor settlers
and those who lay claim   RIP

is this where peace fell? is this where the arrows got broken
two sides collide in deadly dust-up
don't trust the lakes, they have collected the lies of years
in the rain that fell from the sky
the lakes are busy cleansing and processing
the deceit of strangers
recycled back to the sky to fall down again, cleansed
and lifted back up to become a better truth, less lie
the years will make it perfect, the perfect lie

west is best, east is worst, nothing is north
south has red stones
the mountain brushes crumbs from her lapel
sending gravel down, rerouting travellers
news reports nothing the rocks don't already know
and the road bends a little, it sends the dust flying
it wants to stay wide open, it wants to marry the cloud
here, a ten-mile wingspan doesn't even touch the sides
this is forever, the energy expands, never ending
the great mystery will bring you into
who you who you who you
really are – life's a bitch, you needn't fear it

the moon has finished its coffee and is just hangin' around
for the next time to shine, it likes to see things in daylight
compliments the sun when things look good
before waving goodbye tucking in tired before returning
of this we can be sure you needn't fear it

the moon likes to see if anyone will rewrite the legends
wants to hear the stories retold to see if they are still true
can you write about the moon without romance
or righteous moral, something that won't insult
something occult, the moon will approve
it likes all the gossip, it loves to be included
in the glamour magazines
posing in all the pictures with all the stars
the moon won't let us forget her

controlled roads say, "go here, don't go there, follow
no passing, absolutely no passing"
I've got my poems, I've got my sage, I've got my corn
I've got my rocks, I've got the memories that made the poems
I've got the medicine of root
I've got the pictures, I've got my songs
I've got my blanket, I've got my pillow
I've got my sounds, I've got my eyes
I've got my feet, I've got my voice, I've got my fingers
I've got the time change and
the way of it

the people don't speak of land, they speak of the people
who speak of industry that speaks in big fat numbers
but never bigger than
the horizon that holds them
or deeper than the canyons where they'll fall
west-side stories (America KKK) never talks about the land
only commerce and how many times they can
come inside her

Forty Dayz

it beginz
inside
skinz
like hivz
busy beez
pleazing
eazy
harvesting honey
vatz of it
flooding
pouring forth
torrential downpour

pollination
of sensez
tensions
building
brewing newness
business
buzz-ness
bee-ness
cum-ness
creation
cremation

worker
bee-buzz
patience
in time
all secrets revealed
soundzz
that's all
soundzzzz
ZZZzzzz ZZZzz
crownz
QUEENZ

royaltee
She-Bee
chosen
potions and
poisons
Queenie

time change
radiation
gen-med-modification
believe
bee-lie
bee-get
bee-side

teenytinyeenyweeny
littlebittybees

Love Is a Long Moan

There are harmonies in nature
Elements brushing up against
The sound of conflict and friction
Different from lyrical compositions
Filling silent spaces with confessions
Of false love
Wordy political explanations
Excessive talking avoiding
Real meaning
Speaking abysmal English
Contracts in comments
Would you mind repeating

We are the generation of handwritten
Cardboard slogans
Branding solutions and trademarking
Our movements
We are the authors of normal
We said it was okay to eat flesh
We congratulate construction
That holds us up in the name
Of progress
Blasting our way through hard
Rock, let's talk politics

I enjoy a flagless landscape
Somewhere, where no one has lain claim
Somewhere, where Crown land and treaties
Forgot
Make room for
Music, the songs belong to
Sound, birthed from ground
Rising swelling inspiring singers
Looking for answers and lovers
Calmed by loss, touched by melody
Life and death filling
Sky and space

Rub our eyes, everyone
The sun rises for us
We praise the mother
For her strength
Born from necessity
With instincts
We can choose not to clutter
Her with more things
Offspring to prove this power
My love letter looks like
Resistance to conformity
Never torn by choice, I don't mind
If my voice and line end right here

To the right, there is a river
And a ribbon of steel
Running parallel, simultaneously
Both flowing fast to the city
Carrying passengers and appetites
One placed there, one original

Summer earth sweat
Sweet scents, climbing to heights
Eye to eye with giants
Where tricky winds speak in riddles
We listen for voices of long-gone friends
Instead the sound found is internal
It tells us, "We create this normal
We say what is acceptable"
The influence so powerful
Remember Hitler?

Off in the distance the iron bison roars
Reminds us this progress
Combines us, based in a nationalistic
Reality held together by a big
Steel stitch, shifting dollars

East and west, taking from one
And giving to the other
Arriving and leaving

We question people's reasons
For not believing the desperation
That brings them to a place of dishonesty
There is a man in the middle of the bridge
Holding two middle fingers straight up
To the sky, he wonders, "Why"

Trust your instincts™
If it sounds like it
And feels like it
And looks like it
It probably is

We can hardly believe
When the young ones leave us
The eye of the beholder failed us
The dead friend decided
Jumping was just what they needed

Darkness is a tunnel with light at either end

The pain of honest love lost
Is lamented in songs and will be again
Making beauty with urban versions
Of honesty filling the airwaves
Bought in a dead-man's deal
Over a century ago

Stroking the Serpent

Danger!

Nature
Follow
Steps taken
Listen
To the mutha
She sings
All day long
Songs
I've heard before
Sounds
Like oceans coming
To shore
Like hatred
Drowning

We hold people
And suffer
With carelessness
Spiritual conflict
Awkwardly
Ask for answers
Haphazardly
Look for directions
Expect the best
Prepare for the worst

We are approaching
We walk for many days
We are approaching
The house waits in patient emptiness
We are approaching
We are walking
We are approaching

Geography is a two-dimensional
Plane – home page
Elastic words stretching
Meaning so many things
Indifference is born in one place
Two realities, intertwined
Imagined blind divides
Afraid to take a peek inside
The burden of knowing
Gets deflected, rejected by the
Everyday

We are approaching
We are noticing everything
We are telling the stories, willingly
We are carrying keys

Sweetness breaks hearts
Hearts reaching for heights
Feelings
We alone
Cannot inspire
We know
Too much desire
I am biting
The apple
And sitting
Beneath the tree
Waiting
For the lightning
In silence

The walls of the house remember
They are swollen with stories
None of which are true
The house will do this to you
Doubt serves memory like

Winter challenges our survival
The house is far away
We still see it
Together
We are approaching

Two supernovas stumbling
Dropping expectations arriving
Reject neglect, directly forcing
Passions back into boxes
No good
No evil
There are only
Nature's answers
Suspended like fruit from the limbs
Of gracious aged trees
We stroke the serpents
Invite them to dinner
Formidable circumstances
To say the least
We expect miracles
Not magic

What is the sound
Of a mountain
Crumbling
Burying the future
Making so much noise
Like brakes squealing
Like earth-peeling machines
I am saving
All the memorial
Poetry for tomorrow
I keep death at bay
Serving purpose
With agreements made

Long before
The light of day

Come to the house
Come into the house

The world is waking
Outside our doors
Rallies
Forming
Communities moving
Asking
Important questions
Dancing and daring
Attracting attention
This is what fighting looks like
Collective resistance
Gets results
Resolve, commitment
Elevation, vibration

Come home

I Was There

Frothing at the mouth
Making garbled conversation
Swallowing meaningful messages
Before they have a chance to float
Words slide right down
The river's throat
Ricochet off rocks
Survive forgetfulness
Stick around
The next show
Is right now

I was there
When the people
Didn't give up
Battling floods and fires
Two contrasts
Half a mile away
From each other
Treading over aftermath
Don't fear the silence of ash
Forest giants go
By way of the buffalo
These ground matters
Don't concern the birds
They perch before searching
New homes in unfamiliar
Places displacing themselves
They change nature's course
Single-handedly and out of
Necessity

Angry currents raise their voices
Together in deafening danger cries
Mercy abandoned this place years ago
Water tempo driven by temperament

The environment in argument
Forces its hand, holding its foot
Looks like shores
Unnatural ten times faster
Than any human stride
Ploughing new courses and yet
Not going anywhere

Build the bridges, conquer the will
Harness the energy of humans
Control fear
Get inspired
We are home
So act like it
Lead by example
Mobilize
Thrive and decolonize
Let go of division
We can remake all of this

Cast a collective eye
See what's here and what's not
We are
Laws of thought
Respectful intention
Recognizing friction within
Helpful tools
Living on ice
And hoping it won't crack

I was there
When we learned new words
And others were invented
When the government stole identities
And we impeached white leaders
Based on infractions

In the 1982 constitutional expression
Section 35, code of ethics

Nobody knows what this means
Just go with it

We are building
Ritual around
Deeds
Creating uniformity
Out of need
Our scrambled freedom
Resulted in too much sorrow
Time to borrow a page
From the Great Laws of being
I am doing this for you
And you are doing this for me

They Leave Their Names All over the Place

It takes fifty years to plough
A path through death-lined roads
Patriotism loves
Functional relationships
Celebrated annually
With flags and anthems
All the colours of the rainbow
Believing the beginning began
With them

It takes four hundred years to undo it
To stop speaking to one another
Counting seasons
By how much can
Be taken
Canoes made of tree people
Brought humans and cotton
In no time
The lovely long-haired maidens
Were wearing calico

We were left eating more than flesh
To keep the agreement happy
Over time paths widened and flattened
Waterways filled like freeways
We made trade, we take pay
We made way, they want to stay
Their rules, their game

Who is left suffering
From discovery envy?
Naming rivers after themselves
Leaving namesakes on landscapes
Indians say we should have killed them
Lost men with a thirst to reach the Pacific
Politely curious white guys

Unapologetically superior
At least the coffee tastes good
While retelling the story
A history filed with clenched fists
Still shaking

2

CULTURE

Forever

Forever
as long as the sun shines upon the earth
as long as the water still flows
as long as the grass grows at a certain time each year
Forever
as long as Mother Earth is still in motion
still in motion, still in motion

It's hard work to maintain the middle row
one line makes I separating sides
they navigate a boat down a similar river
we paddle a canoe packing values
never touching, forever separate
maintaining the course
step-by-step laws of RESPECT
intended to protect sacred relationships

Words from good minds
Guswenta, Two Row Wampum
not treaty like it was told but a non-apology
canoe and Boat Ever Flowing Large Water River
buoyancy beyond democracy
boundaries not borders
the law was not authored in an angry house
of disputes but rather inspired from witness
to cause and effect of free will resulting in greed
and corruption and unlawful things

Protection of our relationship to our mother
not better than the other but something necessary
to exercise caution
careful!
steady!
carry on ...
your side
our side
maintaining the middle row
is most difficult

I is for Indian Affairs
I is for Indigenous
I is for Imperialism
I is for Identity
I is for Iroquois/Haudenosaunee
I is for Incident
I is for Initiation

A league of nations
corresponding through beads on a belt
anyone who thinks beads are insignificant
should try getting them back from a museum
crime minister / prime minister
simultaneous colonization and decolonization
relational trade quasi-kin two sides kept equal
this is women's work

Those mountains didn't build themselves

Forever
as long as the sun shines upon the earth
as long as the water still flows
as long as the grass grows at a certain time each year
Forever
as long as Mother Earth is still in motion
still in motion, still in motion

It's about balance and focus
it's about commitment and loyalty
hard things, put in place
speaking the language of agreement
being included from a distance
peace and respect and prosperity

Do NOT cross that line
we said
DO NOT CROSS THAT LINE

Disruption results in consequences
remember Kanonhstaton Caledonia
remember Gustafsen Lake
remember Ipperwash
remember Oka
rememeber Alcatraz and Eagle Bay
remember Wounded Knee
every day is remembrance day
every day

Ongwehonwe original
a national fabric forming
blessing and protecting
something spiritual
not material but a difficult journey
staying the course better or worse
leaving nothing to debate
constitutional consensus overflowing with intelligence
Peacemaker would be proud

Forever
as long as the sun shines upon the earth
as long as the water still flows
as long as the grass grows at a certain time each year
Forever
as long as Mother Earth is still in motion
still in motion, still in motion
Forever

Here's the Deal

What kind of mathematics degree
Or chartered accountant's certificate
Qualifies someone to come up with
Ten thousand for the first year and three thousand
For every year suffered after that

Who sits at the political round table
And agrees in meetings absent of anyone
Directly affected, who nods their head and says
"Yes, this will do, done."

Does the money offer healing
Can it buy time to reflect or afford
A chance to tell our own stories
Names of perpetrators are saved in separate files
Out of context from the rest
canadian legacies living up to expectations
Neglecting important facts and calling it "truth"

How much money does it take to say
"We're still here after you tried so hard"
After the new trucks
And grandkids trick grandmas dry
They don't understand the humiliation
Of the healing process
Memories so horrible you'd swear it never happened
(*Awful*)

Money
Not a new relationship, nothing reconciled
Dollars to wash our hands with
"You've been paid, now go away"
The dealing of healing sounds like
Cash register receipts and news stories
Spilling into living rooms, taking up space
Investments coming up empty
What did they think it would buy
Happiness?

Five O'Clock

The word "tragedy"
Doesn't even apply
Pitifulheartbreakingpainfulterror
This
Not tragedy

What did they think
Would happen
To the humans
When the very earth beneath us
The place that feeds us ...

Trauma
Postassaulthatefulillness
Results of rape
Ripples of sickness
Directly affected by
Fractures
In the sacred

This is what happens

What did they think
The people would do
I'm sorry, I'm so sorry
For you
For your loss of connection
Come back
At least listen

Born into tragic
Genetics
Proud and powerful
Generations
A kind of
Conception and gestation
Beyond tragic

This is what happens

Hotel Reality

Junkie
I can't stand the grabbing hands
The way they drag me in
Against my will, unwelcomed
Uncivilized addiction
Visions of medicine
Dropping like acid on the skin
Tapping your foot off the beat
But it still feels good
Stuck in a sequence of movements
Static minutes passing to hours
This is how Thursday goes
Drugs don't like independence
They are jealous lovers
Overbearing, they like you bound
Little romance to bring you back
After the breakup, but you do and again
You do
It isn't smoke in your eyes
It isn't blood on your sleeve
This is the itch of psychic knowing
You've got to cop to it
We are all multi-dimensional
With invisible bridges connecting
Us together
I am aware of the pain I caused you
I can see it in the reflection of me
In your eyes looking back at you
And on and on

You beg for the songs to stop
For the drugs to wear off
But there is no one there
To hear you and no one who cares
Emotional safety nets break
Dropping like wet concrete

The artist is to the critic is to the reader
Is to the merchant is to the writer is to the muse
Is to the universe is to the _____
The junkie's line is limited
And critical contributions stop short
Our bones are not old hotels
Mysteriously supporting structures
Overdue for demolition
How do we all make a living?

"The most addicting drug of all is silence"
Sentences walking out of the room
Disappearing down fog-filled streets
Leaving questions on the tongue
Life is not complicated
It is not an acid trip
It is a dream
It is a story made of many
Complexity comes when we try
To cheat our way through it
We are still learning
We make the same effort
To do the same things
They already did
Without success

It is useless to try and alter reality
History brings a well-worn shovel
And backhoe when we try
To bury our lies
Sleep is the only true territory unceded
It is precious and sacred
Please do not disturb
The funny-faced masks
Remind us there is something
Beyond ourselves, pay attention

Everything is energy, everything is commodity
I got what you want
You need what I got
How much? Is the question
Love is a heavy negotiation
With subclauses and loopholes
Waivers you never knew you signed
Pay attention

The junkie will call at all hours
Just to see if you're in, hang up
And call again
Performance is a language
We learn to use every day
This voice is for you
Trouble follows drugs
I want to be a dealer
Just for the money
Quick and dirty
Smoke hash on Christmas
Drop X on New Year's
Brutal is the number
Of lost loved ones
Breaking hearts taking faith
Shaking foundations
Pulling cords messin' with justice
Losing balance
We hold hope when we believe in
Recycled souls
Better luck next time

I tell him of the many wet-faced
Women lining the back
Of the funeral home
When he goes, he says
Nothing

The day Buddha decides to
Commit suicide is the day
I stop writing
Worthlessness is a drug
And it doesn't even
Cost anything

Birds Falling

Ain't it strange?
Tears trigger tears
Sex triggers sex
Death is always death is always death
Sounds of laughter can be
Mistaken tearsdeathsex

Coming back
Looks like buckskin on special occasions
But just because
You slapped turquoise on it
Doesn't give you the right
To wear the feathers

We rarely hold men accountable
And feel deeply
The deception of sisters
Forbidden questions are really
Fear disguised as authority

It was once said
The secret to happiness is this

Connecting is easy
It's like ordering a pizza
Understanding is another question
Deathtosextoliestotears
No question

Don't write anything
Just remember
When the earth shook
All the books fell too
No one there to witness this
And no one knows who's next

The birds turned lazy
They no longer want to fly
But expect to be fed daily
Wait patiently for crumbs

We are preparing
For many more odd things
To take over
We don't know the sounds
Of the sorrow of the tears
That will shape tomorrow
The words are not yet birthed
To define what lies will shape
The coming of days
But trust cinematic answers
This is what we think
Is this what we believe?
Coming back in buckskin
With turquoise and feathers
Cover sex, death, lies, and laughter
Listen to the voice that says to you
"Don't do it"
And answer the voice that says
"You should"

The Celebrity of Famous

(includes list of E. Pauline Johnson
museum objects)

Clay Pipe · Flint Corn · Indian Tobacco · Bark Rattle ·
Curtain Rods · Glass Inkwell · Hatchet · Water Drum ·
Carving of Joseph Brant · Deer Head · Small Scissors ·
Knitting Needles · Buffalo Vertebrae · Miniature Suitcase ·
Sewing Kit …

… essentials for the famous, glamorous, notorious …

Celebrated prominence
You are soooooo money
Attainable opulence
Prominence is gold
Forgive those who want less
Lie, that's right, lie
"You cannot find your 'self' with your Mind"

How much do you want?
What are you willing to do for it?
And what are you going to do?
With it when you get it?

"Ready to Die" for it
Notorious Biggie Smalls
Knows it all in the song
"Gimme the Loot"
Do you get it or do you give it?
Lie down for it
Work it jerk it
Make it to get paid?

There is no self without others
I cannot know who I am without
"Y. O. U."
I am the other one
I am the empty

Reflection
I am the one-man band
Bad guy – trying to do good

Small Shallow Black Dish · Clock in Wooden Case ·
Long-sleeved Vest · Decorated Cardboard Box ·
Chain-link Gold Necklace · Cutting Knife · Silver Teaspoon ·
White Slip · Blue Shawl · Black Skirt · Vase · Hair Comb ·
Heavy Marble Rock · Horsehair Rocking Chair · Pens ·

You know the soulless electric
Euro-trance static yet kinetic?
Who writes that shit?
Does it have a mama?
Or know its dadda?
Is it fabulous famous?
Have I missed it?
It goes
Dum-dum-dee-dum-dum
Dum-dum-dee-dum-dum
Nuh-uh-tawr-ee-uhs
Nuh-uh tawr-ee-uhs
Tawr-ee-uhs, tawr-ee-uhs
Dum-dum-Nuh-tawr-ee-uhs

Serious

Let's look back
Tell that reflection to
Repeat after me

"I am the Best"

"I am lovable"

"It's okay if I suck"

"As long as I suck well"

Strong wrong long
Bigger and bigger and bigger
One part legend
One part leisure
You have to want it
You really have to want it
Producers are drooling
The next new thing
Has arrived

Assorted Millinery · China Dog · Glass Knick-knacks ·
Napkin Holder · Crock Dish · 7 Spoons · 11 Saucers ·
1 Platter · Flowers · Red Velvet Shoes · Black Hand Fan ·
Oil Lamp · Lower Jawbone · Poem, "Just for Today" ·

Just for today I will be happy

**(HAPPINESS COMES IN CURRENCY –
LARGE NUMBERS ON PAPER BILLS)**

Just for today I will try to adjust myself to what is

**(I AM WHAT IS, I AM NOW, I AM WOW,
I AM HOLIER THAN THOU)**

Just for today I will take care of my body

**(DON'T CHA THINK I'M SEXY, DON'T CHA WANNA DO ME –
PAY ME)**

Just for today I will try to strengthen my mind

**(STRENGTH IS FOR THE WEAK, I BUY MY STRENGTH,
IT COMES IN A PILL, MADE FROM THE HEART OF THE
ARCTIC FOX MIXED WITH GINSENG PACKAGED IN EUROPE
WITH LITTLE BABY FOX FACES ON THE LABEL)**

Just for today I will exercise my soul in three ways

(MY GURU SAID I HAVE TOO MUCH WIND ENERGY,
THIS HAS BEEN MY BEST PICKUP LINE, EVER!)

Just for today I will be agreeable

(F-U)

Just for today I will try to live through this day only

(HONEY, THEY'LL BE TALKIN' 'BOUT ME LONG AFTER
I'M GONE, THAT'S WHY I DO ALL THIS CRAZY SHIT)

Just for today I will have a program

(FIRST WE LUNCH, THEN WE SHOP, THEN THE SPA,
THEN DRINKS, THEN MORE SHOPPING, THEN THE CLUB)

Just for today I will have a quiet half hour by myself

(WHAAAAAT?)

Just for today I will be unafraid

(IT'S REGISTERED AND LOADED)

Wheeler Sword · Box of Cards · Black Hat and Black Feathers ·
Death Notice of A. Johnson · Gem Jars · Masonic Apron ·
Deer Horns · Union Jack Flag · Black Wig · Red Purse ·
Brown Bracelet · Manuscript, *The Rift* by Pauline Johnson ·

"Someone has lost to-day, the gilded prize
That years endeared unto Ambition's soul
To-night he bears the hardest agonies
of failure in the race to win the goal."
                    E. Pauline Johnson

The Sexual Revolution Will Be Televised

The politics of the erection
The religious obsession
With the rez-erection
Good girls don't want it
As much as bad boys do
The sexual revolution
Is ready for picking

The policy of the hard-on
The dogma of the ding-dong
The economy of the D-cup
The well-endowed and those
without

The bare-naked Brazilian (so indigenous)
The protocol of the raised pole
The constant negotiation of getting it on

"Why don't you come over"
"Uh, I don't know"
"I'll make it worth your while"
"Got any popcorn"
"I got the hot butter too"
"I just want the popcorn"
"Sure, I'll serve it up, however"
"Pay for my cab?"
"What?"

Make Trade – Not War
Inter-Indian Act
Mixed Race Dirty Talk
Fuck you, you dirty filthy squaw
There'll be bleeding in the teepee
Pounding on the ground
Sending primal sounds
Keeping the ancestors up

The sexual revolution will be televised

The sexual revolution is alive and well and
Kicking the shit out of constipated consternation
It's panting and breathing, moaning and
Moving to the rhythm of the new generation
Bumping and grinding, whining its way to exhaustion

Thought: incoming

The quality of the next generation
Is in direct relation
To the ecstasy of the fantasy of the future
Don't fuck it up!
Measuring pleasures in decibels with calipers
Deciding how far the gaps are between where
We've been and sin
Sounds like acoustic, agnostic
Aquatic freaks
Keep your hands inside the boat

Put a life jacket on that thing

Let's collectively write the ode
To the adolescent hormone
The libretto to the fifty-year-old libido
The sad ballad of the reluctant stiffy
And the monologue to that master of solo sex
Master Bater

Hef said, "All the senses must be in play, boy."
Brain tissue too or Thou Shalt Not
Rewriting new realities with moral authority
Imagine: we can have power over our own bodies
Imagine: we can have authority over our own skin
The sexual evolution will go forward
Follow

The pleasure principle is so individual
Mixed with current cultural keeps this red skin
Hot, we invented this dance
Or have you forgot?

Authent®ick

These are not airport gifts
Or museum objects
These are dreams of spirit
Plucked from thin air
With colour and thought and breath
These are reclamations
Stuck to them with humour
These are visual medicine
These are good food
These marks
Are made for you

It took many collected minutes
Rather than one fell swoop
When "tradition" gradually opened up
Definitions and the painters
Gingerly followed suit
The moment cannot be measured
When artists began to
Break
The moulds to tell the public
It is different than what's been told
This mislearned history,
Mind-bending reality
They loop us through designs
Like psychedelics in duplicates
New traditions fast transforming
Bridges and tunnels
Freudian fantasies put in print

The road from past to present
Is not long and linear
It circles fast towards the finish
Where it begins travelling again
Backward to find the next new thing
Interpretation, acceptance, encouragement

Practice, elastic, fantastic
Electric
Red
Black
Black
Grey
Grey
White
White
Red

Just ask

What am I looking at?

Traditional

Spiritual

Cultural

All the loose-lipped language
Floating like orphaned words
Ungrounded from meaning
Serpents eating their tails
Swallowing definitions until
Like the totems left in natural habitat
All but disappear to reappear as thick
Forest muck on boots
Tracked through sterile gallery floors
Interpreted as disrespect

Uncultured imbeciles

Stories as strong talk along with
A song and a dance
Smile
The photographer still
Deals in souls

Red-Black

Red lives
outside confines of lines
too thin to hold bold sexy expression
canvas white stained and stretched
ripped open wounds
lace forever stamps of
fiery hot honey blood drops
liberated along
roadways bending guidelines
unencumbered finding ways
to meaning, seemingly easy
trickery

Less lines – more truth
absent of secondary and tertiary boundaries
First Nations flavours
loaded with innuendo
presto chango
just when the experts thought
they had this thing nailed
to the wall
along comes Raven
dancing on fresh concrete
wearing masks in Holy Houses
playing knick-knock on
wooden boxes

Black
Raven's last fantasy
he hiccups confessions
mussing his feathers
gulping languages almost extinct
burping biblical verses
polluting the air
with curses

Black can't be bought
but wants to be paid all the same
no shame in a tap dance and a story
so long as what's sacred stays sacred
the consumer wants to understand that

Black is tension teasing you
to come closer
listen to the poetry inside the silence
money does not speak or gesture but
commands the lands
it divvies up space
stitches it back together
calling it policy
Art comes from a place
of imagination floating down
rivers of trust, rising and swelling
with secret ambition
never wishing to be anything
but art

We are the stars of our own stories
glowing against a night sky
held together by a grand blank canvas
Creator winks, and suddenly nothing
is the same
change gonna come
change gonna come

We gather to witness unions in galleries
Red-Black Life-Death
a river and a waterfall
intelligence and heart
married in a civil service
by artist and audience

Witness

When God speaks of art
She uses lots
Of hand gestures
Strikes the air with invisible lines
But never describes colour
Except to say
"Feel it"

Tolerant laws
And mandated methods
Of reconciliation
Do not change the
Relationship or our responsibility
To remain

Influence
Spreads within the mainstream
With myths of broken traditions
Offering history as solutions
The how and the why
Finding answers in textbooks
College level responses of
Of non-extinguishment

The political, personal, professional
Fuse and find one another
Move along the same planes
Across landscapes where
Colonial competition breeds
Corporate norms
Seduction of the material
We want coffee
We want war
But we'll take credit
And plenty of it

Our presence is
Powerful enough
Confusing enough
Validating enough
Disturbing enough
In our wordless stillness
We offend
And this
Is a gift

In the same way we get away
With a lot by calling it dancing
We can say so much inside paintings
Overhearing well-intended
Whispers questioning
"How do they come up with this stuff"
This stuff is no one's job to tell
Or promote better understanding
It is constant and exhaustive

This is the original songwriter
Making music with just a drum
This is paint used to articulate
Collective experience
Instigators as artists
Risk takers taking risks
Committing subversive acts
Selling them back
As non-colonial constructs
Individual trophies promoting
Corporate separateness
Survivors feeling familiar breezes
Sending chills of remembrance
Alone in an answerless echo

Like measuring disturbance
And displacement by dropping

Indigenous art in the middle of
Contemporary pools, what is left
Is the weight of what is offered

When God speaks of art
She never points to where words
Do not suffice but mixes colours
To reflect the people
Drawing us inside the circle

We Are Swimming

In gene pools
Floating on liquid skins
Reconnecting to water
Flirting with weightlessness
Touching one of the elements
Holding our history
We welcome young ones
Teach them to float
We are swimming with communities
We are dreaming of being
Here, and here we are
Crossing together through the tunnel
Trusting directional instincts
Shifting from one side
To the other
Patiently waiting fidgeting with
Our own importance
Troubling inconvenience when refused passage
The gift of go and float
Stop and play
Transforming landscapes reflecting us
Constructing agreements from collective truth pools
Architects and artists
Visionaries and cashiers

We are swimming
Decisions forming
Past generations crossing trestles
Vantage points, pointing
Future possibilities shaping
Placing measures
Perfection and pride
To say
"Hey look, we are swimming"

Sky Woman Falling (a POV blog)

Part 1

I have the world in my belly
the air pulls me uncontrollably.
I don't care about the growing gap
separating my husband and me
strangely, I don't care.

I am already falling like Alice into a wonderland.
Here I am fighting and befriending "air."
I am as weightless as an astronaut.
I am an autumn leaf
so this is freedom.

This is freedom of flesh and emotion.
So this is where ancestors leave to
circle round to meet you again.
My husband, my unborn, her unborn
this is where we'll know everything.

Everything is all around me.
Am I moving or am I
being moved.
I hope this never ends.

I am gravity's puppet.
Away. I am going away and arriving.
I have to remember this.
I have to remember to breathe.
I see something.

I am the wingless angel.
The shoeless traveller.
A woman with answers packing instincts.
Speed is increasing.
This falling stops.

I am caught. The geese have me.
My, how they are graceful and look at me
curiously.
I see something far off.
Could that be
my future?

Sky Woman Falling (a POV blog)

Part 2

The rushing air cradled her like a hammock.
She slept and dreamt
wild restless dreams
more vision
less prophecy.

All the colours spun together
to make white from black
sounds and songs.
A natural soundtrack of spiritual tones
moving outside, inside her.
Inspiring indescribable knowing
evolving growing like life.

There is no escape.
This fate is in play.
She felt the weight
and responsibility crushing reality.
She slept and dreamt
of opposite things unwild and unaware.

Dropping.

Her loose limbs pointing
upward towards her home.
Her home, never more.

Just falling.

The winged ones seeing and saying
"Look, a sky woman is falling."
Others warning, "Do not interfere."
And a confrontation was had.
The sun and moon took it into consideration.
It was then decided.
The geese beings would hold her in place
suspended while they arranged for an earth-body to house her.

A home, where she would be placed and left alone to live
out her will.

Sky Woman Falling (a POV blog)

Part 3

I AM WIDE AWAKE.

The creature family worked hard for me.

All the water now released from me
and the pain has begun.
They work with urgency
the little ones.
They know another one comes.

The earth beneath me grows as if with every breath
and I am clutching something.
There in my palm are seeds
I've never seen before.

New dreams brought me here
and I must trust
and embrace the pain
of the coming of this new one,
a sister ally.

The new world is expanding
I am landing, leaving, and arriving.
I am coming, I have gone.

The wind commands my hand
the same time the girl comes forth
and those alien seeds leave – scattered in a chaotic gust.
Both are born, woman and man.
Never alone again.

We are the people.
My girl joins me on the soil.
The earth is witness to her birth.
Land memory has begun.
Layers built on feelings.

Home. I am home.
I made it.

Love and Protection

Love and protection look like
Love looks like
War looks like
Protection looks like
Respect looks like
Love looks like
Resistance
Looks like
Trouble looks
Like lessons
Looks like
Answers ·
Looks like
Vigilance

Acceptance independence
Dangling faith on the end of a stick
Shining white in the face of the enemy
Starting over and over and over and over
Walking in trust blind trust through ego-less
Paths recycled concepts revisited
Carpets of golden knowing awakened
Sacrificial gravitational beings wearing
Weighty hefty identities cultural knowledge
Song slingers sounding out sturgeons swimming
Together gathering working towards what end

Heaven is a place, an individual happening not
Writing but remembering total inspiration dancing
Circles

Respect and knowing look
Like knowing respect looks
Like speaking looks like
Sharing looks like challenging
Looks
Like sober looks

Like shaping and naming looks
Like separate looks
Like application and practice
Looks like
Failing looks
Like the moon falling
Looks
Like them
Looks like us
Looks like
Sixty extra pounds
Looks like bells born
In the ground looks
Like men
Looks
Like overlapping
Happening

Conjured up contrasting
Corruptions keeping vigilance
Through reproduced ceremony
Only to understand fractions and pass on
Notions of the original but practised
With authentic faith, facts tucked between
Pages and sold to no one in particular
No one who knows what to do with it
No one goes to extremes anymore
No body is the best identity, anonymous artist
No thing separate always
With us

Shining constantly shining the light
Dissect the sacred till nothing
No thing can live above the sun
Below
there's a billion blazing taxis raising a roar

Stealth and presence look
Like stealth and presence
Looks like presence
Look presents
Like presence
Looks
Like secret presents
Looks secret looks
Present

3

POETRY

3rd Stone from the Sun

Jimi says
open your mouth, swallow this
are ... you ... experienced
it's getting late so much earlier
the sun sets inside the earth
glowing with rhythm
resounding sunshine
blowing my mind to bits
he who throws the first stone
takes down the gate
passes through without answers
we never earned the right to know
but take it
just the same
we are e. x. p. e. r. i. e. n. c. e. d.

Jimi says
prama*mowa*noojup*tik*foo
speaking in tongues
silver-forked vocables
not quite poetry
but poetry
just the same
we create a place where words
have no say
where sound makes shapes
pictures plastered on landscapes
intelligent teachings from sun beings beyond
man! are we peaking?
this terrific poison
bringing us closer into focus
I think I'm in love
I think I am love
I am love
I love
love

whooooooowh
it wasn't long before we
unlocked the rocks
released them from sleep
inside disturbances
so natural and necessary
we climbed down the cosmic ladder
opposite of never-ever land
throwing the 2nd stone
for luck
into fountains

Jimi says
make a wish
and I tell him the same thing
I say when the stars fly by
"make us aware"
once we are there
we can't go back to unaware
whooooooowh
together we grasp a staff
extending as far above as below
make a connection to
something like lightning
hateful hostilities released
compassions compelling our souls
the 3rd stone
waits
patient and pretty
we boomerang round
the sun
meet our future at the beginning
the same one lived yesterday
broken stones, hurt nothing
whoowh

Used to Be (Home)

hard, horny
dirty ol' trails

a city of shallow breaths
slippery steps
conductors and three-dollar
transfers
slower than dreams coming true

a city of dark-alley dwellers
offering limousine pleasures
acid baths
continual construction
this could be anywhere
nowhere new

forced concentration
stay on track
a hundred-dollar
ride to the top
a sawbuck to get across
dead memories
numb

when all it took
to stop sinning was to stop sinning

multicoloured cultural
Cold War countries living as neighbours
lampposts of hope
food stamps and food banks

where are the songs?

offerings piled up and flushed down
dual debris
cruel sleep too brief
no relief come morn

survivors learn to lean
into change
find ways to live, lie, or leave

where is the sun?

We Are

we are listening with
open hearts
trespasses forgiven
we are well-fed plentiful nations
remembering messages
grateful for warm shelter
and shared abundance
with the lesser blessed

listen to rhythms speaking
our connection to **Creation**
happy fire lives inside
as **New Year's** resolutions
we are delivered
from familiar dark places
rise up keep climbing
we are born
without limits
we know
the other world
waits for our work to
be done

we walk
together towards it
lessons in love and struggle
packed inside
I am you and we are
everything born
to be kings and queens upon
the earth's kingdom

we are wind
breath, not dragon fire
but the same immortal

mythical magic flows
swiftly as ocean waves
of change and strange messages
bringing sparks of thought

take care to travel with
family flames leading you back home
every time as beacons reach
into dark universes
looking for **origin**
it stopped

the knot undone
footprints fingertips
lips limbs lost
the calls stopped
tough-skinned responses
healing minute by minute
recapturing
nurturing honesty
hummingbird returns
reminds us
smile
broken-hearted warriors
walk forward
keep walking towards
tomorrow
embracing recovery
lighting forest fires
reciting prayers
taking their place
and when ready
walk alone
ravens visit
deceased relations

reborn as light **Creation**
reminds us remember
wounds closing words consoling
wondering if emptiness is obvious
blemishes on records forever

it stopped

Reject, Rejection, Accepted

Fire and steam, determination and steel
mixed races, bosses, and slaves
slave bosses take it just a bit further
a different city promises
snakebite oils
easy-come
easy-go
dreams

Part 2

What's it got to do
with you
fifty years' experience
black is the new black
more disturbance of the peace
(outdated) laws locked up
the wrong criminals wear it
on a T-shirt for justice
all war and all sport are homoerotic acts
experimental outlets for
sexual aggression seeking peace
and solution through the spilling
of another's blood
oftentimes heroes are unable to
stand alone

Chorus

Paper and gold
one will save you, the other will fool you
the words aren't coming, you have to
go get them. They hide in the streets
that's where you'll find them

Chapter 3

Sounds of jazz with a plunky bass
follow the plot to obvious ends
it's not like life. We can't make predictions
trouble and lovers take us back
ten years, when memories used to take
up so much time wasted and regretful
open wounds healing over miles
they couldn't stomach a truth
that didn't fit the profile so renewing
citizenships never came into question
reject, rejection, accepted

Act 2, Scene 4

Outdoor, midday, rain.
the boys unstick their boots
from a puddle of mud and carry on
they have ten cents each and wish for
cherry bubble gum, black licorice
and chewy green jujubes
reward is a one-hour walk away
towards tinsel and overweight comfort
behind the counter, elders, overly kind
someone who knows their story and forgives them
little brown boys believing sweets
make them equals they speak
with beautiful cheekbones
and almond-shaped eyes
they are "locals"
the beginning of handsome looks like this

P.S.

Prejudice hangs in the air like thick pollution
racists less obvious breathe deep convictions
traditions are practised without question
balance and justice are suiting up again

fighting back again
put up your dukes let's dance
this one out
again

Let's hear your knuckles crack
let's see you roll up your sleeves

Fight for peace

He Ain't Comin' Back

Walt Disney thinks his frozen body
can awaken when it thaws
when all the dollars
intended for cancer research
are actually used
for cancer research
and he can be cured

Walt Disney could have
cured cancer
with all the dollars
it costs to keep
his soulless body
on ice

he's not coming back
he's not Jesus Christ

his legacy is a three-fingered
rodent who had no answers
no grain of intelligence
no teachings for the children
Bukowski was appalled
that America should love
a soulless thing, created
by a frozen man
believing in soulless things

I don't like
the Dalai Lama
I can't understand him
it's not his accent, I just think
he makes no sense
he hasn't fucked up his life
and circled back
he hasn't earned the right
to tell me anything

my grandma
has a rattle
she shakes it
I feel it
heal me
the sound moves
one side
to the other

my grandma
has a rattle
and one day
I will too

given the chance
as if
we'd ever wanna come back
at all
exist like mist playing
plasmatic peekaboo
don't be a fool

release your soul, Walt Disney
can ya hear me?
you ain't doing anybody any good
taking up space in the freezer
ya stupid human ice cube
in time global warming's
gonna get you too
In time
all the body-filled earth cavities
will host signs that say
Full up Today
Come Back Tomorrow

Sap

he
served
me tree
sap in a shot
glass I stretched
my neck to get
every drop

he
served
me tree
sap in a shot
glass I stretched
my neck to get
every drop

he
served
me tree
sap in a shot
glass I stretched
my neck to get
every drop

he
served
me tree
sap in a shot
glass I stretched
my neck to get
every drop

Bearskin

Protection
Shaman
Burdens – blessings
Raising questions
Elevations
White raven – mysticism
Collections

Wooden rings
Cedar wings
Feathers and flutes
Convolute
Magnificent magical masks
Beads
And shells
Healing spells
Tell
Your tale
And make it tall

Pacific creations
Anticipation
Giants and thunder
Dancers
Make a pact
Spiritual contract
Sprung back
Dug up
Labelled
Enabled
Awesome
Sauce

Can't wait

Forgetting
Remembering
Try

Lying
Smoking
Wishing
Give it away
Time travelling
Tornado-ravaged homes
Pushing the envelope
Can't wait
Sign-language tutors
Excellent movie reviews
Gone off
The depends
Aurora borealis
Fine-feathered phallus
Curious destinies
Supernova
Dust clouds
Reflector shades
Powwow
Slow burn
Quick learn
Running for the border
Cancer dancer
Switch hitter
Perfectionist
Patience
Numbskull
Handsome, dark, and tall
Strangers
Sound-bite bullets
Conscience decisions
Poking at the wound
Starving the disease
Stinging in the rain
Poverty

Can't wait
Can you?

Hang It on a Hook

Enter
There was a time
When all it took
Was a look
All it took
Was time
When all it took
Was feeling the fire
And knowing

Now
Our forces are left
Wondering
Our powers go
Keep go- go- going
And answers
Can no longer find us
We feel the pressure
Of purpose
And faith takes us
With patience
Leading

Enter
The idea
Of creation
In everything
We are life giving
And life taking
The womb is the moon
Of the orbit we spin
This fantastic ecstasy
With words, and songs
With lives and thought
The mundane, given permission
To live to take to give
Today

Freedom
Is no small thing
It is the essence of us
Sky Woman fell
But did not fear
We stumble like
Stars dropping
Connecting with friends
Who stumble too
This isn't losing
We are fulfilling
A way laid out for us
To know the pain
Embrace the pleasure
Answer to no one
Disconnect and reconnect
Envision

"Righteousness is never lost forever
unless one casts it away oneself"

Open
We already know
What we need to know
We have already lived this
'Tis better to have loved and lost
'Tis better to ingest experience
Than to walk away clean

Return
Talking woman to woman
The powerful pleasure
Improving the universe
One mind at a time
Bringing buckets of intelligence
To the table and feasting

Nurturing back into being
Natural woman
Fire woman
Free and righteous woman
Return

Awake Awake

Fear is a familiar vernacular
Listen to the expression
We breathe in and out
The pollution in unison
Bubbles beneath us shake upward
Like earthquakes opening
Sending aftershocks, impulsive
Happiness until low frequency
Is no longer an option

We were supposed to be listening
Instead we were looking beyond
Voices sounding satisfied
It's not technology's job
To point us towards
The future, uncertainty keeps
The conversation alive
I'm removing "if" from my
Vocabulary because what is, is

The rivers you knew as a child
Are still recognizable for now
They never end
But transition into bigger bodies breathing
And the songs play on long
After sunset creating exciting territory
For romance and intuition

The surreal feeling of being
Out of control in the midst of so much beauty
Sweet sound-songs float to match the magic
Acts made of nothing but light
Poof
Now you see it ...
Realizing the earth is part of a universe of
Chance forces absorbed into one another
We hold on to wonder

Breaking like thunder
Speaking its power

Light slips gradual we grasp
Desperately before it's all gone
What is left to say, we never say
Offer instead laughter and proper
Behaviour more than ever knowing
Shadow is born from light of day, awake

Surprise Me

We have ash falling between our fingers

No domain left to claim no heaven
To hold us
Men walk clumsily among queens
And choose to behave as they do
Surprise me

Even greed-ravaged lands
Still hold songs and real
Physical experience
"Death," she said
Is a lot like sleep
Stay awake awhile with me
Witness natural patterns breathing
In and out narratives
People and conflicts and
Threats and plots
And people and places
And connections and inspiration
Think it all over – tell me a story
Make my day – surprise me

Pick a side
You must choose the difference
That defines you
Determination defies gravitational laws
Buoyant spirits have a hand
In our existence
Suspended disbelief like fantastic
Fiction, we have written many endings
But neglect to remember
Spell the word and use it in a sentence

Trust and justice and truth
Miss the days when they used to be
One and the same
Heart matters climb ladders

To get a better look over the hill
Where they used to play wild and free
With honest friends
Now retreats in regretful defeat
Allowing untrue stories three times removed
To rename and reshape
Wrapped up in a lot of gossip

We extend a hand where commerce fails
With glowing hearts we hear the cries
Rise like ghost voices on loose layers
I am not now, nor have I ever been
What I am not, I will be as needed
To be when needed
I am one side of many, there are plenty of
Options luring your loyalty
And the choices all sparkle with integrity

We live in total dysfunction
And accept shortcomings without question
We sleep with and awaken from discomfort
I can't tell the difference between the two sides lined
Up like soldiers no distinctions apart from the other
Assumption loves assimilation
Separation is a fallacy, we are living in each other's laps

Choice holds hands with freedom and rights are born
Holding worn-out flags
Stand by me at all times
Choose to do this without doubt
Just pick a side, surprise me
Speak your words and defend them
Spit back regurgitated words left on doorsteps
Like abandoned babies
The soundtracks don't match the actions
When we are left wondering
Which one is the hero

Do
Be fantastic
Ask trick questions

Dig deep to plant your convictions
Burn down the forest and make your way
Through

Alotta Hullabaloo

Grouchy Conservatives
Didn't get enough liquor
At the last convention
And began to take it out
On the Indians, complaining
"All they want is handouts
Probably spent their whole life
Living off of my tax dollars"
Then shut down hate sites
Before giving time to retort

Things change, slowly
Sometimes overnight
But never do they not
Like my friend said
"Wait long enough, and
Shit happens."
He's married and divorced
Shit sure happened to him

Convention
So much done in the name of it
Convention, considered tradition
But not like how Indians define it
Repetition, like Americans
Coming north once a year
To get the good deals

Rich people look weird
They don't look like themselves
They look like they let
Someone else dress them
And comb their hair
Seventy-five per cent of voters are over sixty-five
No surprise
They are the ones who climbed
When the ladder was still stable

They believe in the system
That built their homes and
Padded their retirement
They see nothing wrong with
Plastic and potato chips

But enough of "they" and "them"
"Us" and "we"
Everyone is a miracle
Young and old and medium
I don't hate Conservatives
I just don't like their fashion sense
Can spot 'em a mile away at a protest
I confess
A house would be nice
Placed on a hill
Where birds fly by
And clouds manipulate themselves
Into abstract compositions, a garden
Some pets, a place for the bumblebees

How much is this gonna cost me
How many poems will it take
To build my house

A State of Mine

Heavy Indian cheeks lift
Flat brown feet shift
Hungry lungs expand
And take in toxic salt
Dark eyes stay arrow-straight
Forgiveness lives on the streets
Politeness comes across
As caring, compassion, and healing
The city is still crying but it is trying
To hide the tears
Signs say Welcome
Hard sidewalks are still long
The towers still tall
No need at all to build another
The womb of this mother has given
Resiliency through celebrity
There is love in New York City

Psychic detection swirls
Three hundred and sixty
Eyes ask for passports
Mine is brown, and solid
Feet on the ground
The Spanish ladies ask
But I cannot tell

The beating this city's been taking
Is not weakening the palpitating
The scaffolding is holding
Not only the history
But what is to come
Old bones groan below
Man-made shores can not stop
The waters, the Hudson hides
Its original name we claim
The river we rescue its meaning
From oblivion

Crossing intersections as negotiations
Collaborations, events, and expensive
Street lights are only suggestions
Do as you will, do as you can
Pass with caution, look ahead
Safety is a spirit that follows
Only so far, allows us to make mistakes
And leaves unexpectedly

"I love New York" has new meaning
Bigger than the White House–sanctioned
Camo-clad military protection
It comes from the citizens
Who perch themselves along
The boardwalk just to have the chance
To tell their story, promote their pride
Stake their place in a rich history
So it's not forgotten, not wanting
Dollars, but a chance to relive it all
In laminated pictures, telling us of
The changes that have claimed one corner
Of the whole. One angel among many
Administering medicine with salty
Stories of yesterday, a moment in time
Remembered forever

Humidity swells between concrete
Corridors, sits still and motionless
As liquid barrios
Affections are negotiated connections
Expressed as cautious, not careless generosity
Knowledge and eligibility go the distance
In the vast/fast city given way
By the river that flows both ways

What is the future of our shorelined lady?
They admit there have been storms and more

Are coming, they must prepare, not as
Military but as elders of their own
Pull forth knowing from within
Rely on self and help others
Sisters listen to instincts and the mothers

4

POLITICS

Louder than Ever

They are hosting
A funeral for something
Not yet dead and singing
Celebration songs from the homelands

We are breathing
Long deep breaths
Between the lines of our
Oratory of inspiration
We listen

They were hoping
It'd all be over
By the new year
Able to shake off flakes
Of residual history
Still clinging to our coattails
Of survival

We are singing
Louder than ever
Passing pride down the line
Giving thanks for schools and churches
Teaching us distrust and resistance
We appreciate it

They appear perplexed
Every time we rise
Letting it sink in, for just one second
They could have been taught lies
Dismissive pursed lips
They swallow

"Look what they're doing over there!"

This is the food we've been craving
We are filling our spirits and we are gorging
On this goodness

Move a Mountain (Walk a Mile in Her Shoes)

We want more
And we want it now
We want it to stop
And we want it to stop now

Lies are violence
Stop telling lies
And holding back facts
There is only truth
And you know this
We know this
We feel it
Truth is a choice
So choose it
It will set you free
Freedom
Is worth it

We are survivors
With many scars
Lined along body territories
Brought together making
Road maps that look like Turtle's back
This land mass, our home, where sisters
Go missing, we miss them
This physical place so disconnected
We hear them call to us
They keep calling to us

Come back, sisters
To the teepees and lodges
Come back, aunties
To the big houses and wigwams
Come back, grannies
To the deep forest lean-tos
Come back, clan mothers
More than ever, we need you

Walk proud
Let your steps resound
Travelling down into the
Earth where my grandmother
Sleeps and yours does too
We knock on her door and say
"Show us the way
Teach us the words
Feed us knowledge and
Reconnect us to the earth"

Criminalized catastrophes
Make headlines every time
The time it takes to keep
Us safe takes up so much
Hours better spent collecting
Beautiful lessons and blurring
The lines between us until
We begin to move together
Venturing outward under
Magical moonlight without
Worry of darkness or danger
Running in celebration through
Light-filled fields
This need for protection
Produces so much distraction
Makes my head and body
Ache with exhaustion
Stay calm, reclaim your place

If we could really walk in her shoes
We wouldn't be walking at all
But running for our lives
Running with the wolves

We stand and watch
Calendars roll over

Into another year
Without resolution or solution
We see elders translate for Creator
In folded-armed stances they ask
"You don't know war is wrong yet,
You haven't stopped the violence?"

The movement moves one step to the next
We make it our business to correct it
Expand our minds to the endless possibilities
It looks like razor-sharp wit
And feels like fire flares
Sounds like heartbeats on the ground
So you better walk loud
Because
There is nothing more powerful
Than a naked woman
Standing in nothing
But her intoxicating beauty
Her gorgeous forthrightness
Her strength to protect those she loves
No weapon can penetrate this

Action.
Our survival is political
Action
We walk
With intention
Our legacy
Is us, living
As examples
Agents of change
Moving in unison

It is time, it is time
To move, move
Move the mountain.

Eleven, Eleven

eleven, eleven, eleven
sounds like heaven
feels like lucky bones
lucky heavy eleven
remembering veteran
victims
nationalism
fighting unknown forces
standing on stolen territories
robbed in other wars
lucky
eleven, eleven
sounds so fantastic
puts ease in our hearts
brings purpose
to our lives
on rainy days
after earthquakes
we stop stand still
for two, for once
the way they honour
everyone agrees
silence is the best offering
reflection sinks in
beating connections
hearts being
just being
choosing to believe
this choice was given
lives not taken
on eleven, eleven

questions scream
why, why, why
touch
a flag

kiss
a wreath
build monuments
to honour
obscene history
greed
propped up
on a pedestal
death tolls
the bell
eleven
eleven
eleven
this decorated day
some phony-baloney
ceremony
takes shame
and parades it through
the war-won streets
they do it again and
again
remembrance
never remains

Who's Your Daddy

A nation doesn't mind sacrificing
What doesn't make it money
The Crown sits stubbornly saying
"What a shame" and continues to
Breed blindly more of the same

Carlin screams, "Only in America
Is there a disease where people don't
Want to eat!"
Harper heard him and turned deaf
To the defence of Spence's forty-four-day diet
His reply is silence

Makes anger outta comfort
Acts so radical, blame cast to soil
Big business says, "Do unto others"
We don't need your permission
Poisoned attention immigration's
Greatest contribution
The water is tepid where we tread
But wait, come summer
Rivers rage and those No Trespassing signs
Get carried away with the rest

You see, none of this
Is ours

Passing the bar and learning
The language hasn't changed a thing
They win votes in shameful
Meaningless meetings
Eyes opening in saucer-sized surprise
Those double-dipping living
In Indian jurisdiction are mistaken
Brokers don't know how to
Credit their losses
Unseen forces, both positive

And negative, fight like
Brothers to take the lead
In everything
They call their friends
Darkness and fear
Hope and determination
Commanding circumstances
By who can make the masses
Believe in them the most

Second chances granted, turns to
Third and fourth times repeated, equals
Continual suicidal, self-destructive
Obvious from the outside
Does life need be so difficult?
Not sentimental, but historical
Short-sighted efforts
Born from selective memory
Barrelling towards an ultimate end

They'll talk and get it all wrong
These reasons for life interrupted
Secrets taken to the grave
And we
Are fascinated by the repetition
Like seasons and populations
Depleting and increasing

Stay on your toes
Tomorrow's episode
Promises excitement, drama
Dancing bears in costume
We can let the comedians sort
It all out, have them feed it back
To us as clever material
Stories making funny
Because it's all true

Acts of Emancipation

for the Maritime Museum

Justice is careless
And words lose meaning
Without ceremony
Reflective of origins
New traditions
Would see men
Swing
History
Lives in a house
Cobbled together with
Fear and conflict
So much waiting patiently
As ghosts left breathing
Briefly lonely
And unavenged
Statements intertwined
Like braids making rope
Waving in the wind.

Connecting back while pushing
Rocks away from caves
Entering like heroes in Hollywood
Complete with capes
Floor-length, to sweep
The corners of frozen
Spaces collecting particles
Of disconnected time.

Singing new songs
Resonating with new sounds
Dethroning those
Paid handsomely who
Never learned the difference
Between storytelling and lying.

Sighs of sorrow breathing
From souls, those
Who stood witness
To this gasp and cry
Over laws unfamiliar with the land
But born in a man's mind
Foreign policies brought home.

This
Is more than protest
This is more
Than healing
This is much more than
Politics
This is not entertainment
This may look like
Ceremony
This may be
Ritual
This is
Necessary.

We slip through
On quiet canoes
Finding our way
By light
And sound
Over courses
Never chartered
Open instincts
Go.

All the walls
Were touched
Where spirit
And wood
Fused into

New vibration
Invitations
Of cultural voices
Never before spoken
Making rooms ache
With memory echoes.

A digital history
Lives, absent of life
No more safe
From deletion
Than the foreign
Handed-down blanket
Apology.

The inconvenience
Of justice touches us all.

New ghosts walk over
Bloodstained cobblestones
The wind tunnel whistles
Fancy songs leaving
As fast as they fly in
Rain returns
As words unspoken
Hoping more is
Understood

Transformation has begun
And will continue
To ripple into
Years to come
Rescued spirits rest
And now have new ways
To say ...

Giving a Shit

We'll give them leather and feathers
Whatever gets their attention
We'll give them drums and songs
To see how long they'll wait
For us to turn angry

We work with unseen forces
Less a weapon with fewer choices
Our answer to NO MORE. What now
Simultaneous exhaustion
And exhilaration
Determination thick as
Mineral-rich soil negotiations

Not a mob, we are
Peaceful, loving people
We are the timber
Standing in the way
Getting ready for the grave
How close to death
Do they want us to come
Close enough to smell
What it smells like
We have the answers
And we're showing you
Holding them up for your
Glowing hearts to see

Have you nothing to say

The women in their jingles
The fellas in their jackets
The elders in their blankets
And the children
Waving signs
No More, No More, No More, No More

Flags flowing like winter snows
Hands joining in a blizzard of solidarity
I see my people many shades of the same
We are the responsible incorrigible
Bravery in our veins fed by hunger
In our souls, writing love letters
In the snow and messages of S.O.S.
We are revisiting wampum
We are witnessing commitment
Not legislated by war
Or defence budgets
This is the people's love
For the mother
The movement has just begun

Bring it in
Send it out
Walk it around
Sing it loud
Keep it breathing/beating
Resist the hate, keep praying
We are armies of good minds
Ancestor allies walk with us

Blissful ignorance
Sounds like holiday songs
on a Saturday morning
The same day she is starving
For her people
Starving for attention
When the answers are
Within and upfront
Protect, react, resist
Protect, react, resist
Protect, react, resist

So what can I do?

I'm going to fuck
With your money
I'm going to talk
To your children
Tell them the truth
And influence their reality
It's not possible to love a country
And not love its laws
When the law says
A country is formed by
A council and registered
Like a baby's birth certificate
Within the courts the same racist
place that makes the laws,
so what came first?

Is the UN knocking at your door?
Or the ghosts of those
who circled your abode?
Are you finished dreaming of bacon?
Are you begging for protection?
Shaking under a blanket hiding
From your own ancestors saying
"Don't shame us"

Crossing the line – getting close
Closing the gap – moving in
Finding the light – standing in it
Making the sounds – painting in colour
Getting it right – taking names
Planning for the future – reclaiming us

Releasing the medicine – pounding the drums
Staying connected – stepping forward
Rooted in humanity – giving a shit

Reproducing history – recognizing equals
Slam-dancing – gathering
Letting the answers find us

Saying your piece – providing
Helping the cause – craving
Stealing home – forcing the point
Attending to details – walking together
forward …

Is It Easier to Move from Indian to Acculturated Eurocentric Assimilated Brown Skin?
Or the Other Way Around?

Same as the moon
Different from man
Not a war maker
And never complimented
Life giver limited ability

Looking like a star
Falling
Knowing death like a friend
Often silent
Light looks like this
Half and whole all at once
Identity is ready
Connected to forces
Above, below, and around
She
Has a country and named it
Hiawatha where no flag pierces
The land, it sits unclaimed
Ready to serve a common
Purpose, spirit called us
To come

We live on the other side
Of privacy after practical
Matters are exhausted
Inside tragic circumstances
Our real selves are tested
To be revealed with sympathetic
Voices and doing what gets done
Reality consists of this
Dysfunction thrives on lives
Lived outside ourselves
Blessed with less knowing
Our true selves

There can be no separation
Between personal and political
The socialized male emotional conditioning
Makes babies into brutes
Unchargeable assaults walking
The streets as casual as can be
We are dying of sexually assisted ignorance
We function with nuggets of understanding
There is enthusiasm among settlers
They learn to use the language to
Trick each other, cast the hook and
Reel it in

Remove the shoes protecting your soul
Disconnect the connection
Let the blisters heal over
Let the blood dry behind you
This is not fun but a good story rarely is
Feel where it comes from tell it like it is
Where do we put our prayers without land
Are we not real?
Laws of compliance and adherence
Make mutants of us
There is no life without freedom
Of mind, body, and spirit
We are broken people breaking laws
Designed to confine us to violation
We are going to kill the names
They came here with and rewrite
With original language referencing
Positioning not people

Don't believe a story that does not begin
With person, place, and time
This is a legacy in words archived for
The future it is a grand experiment

To witness what we see and what
Is really here
I give you permission to at least
Make mention news you'd like to share
From your corner and go ahead
Ask any question

What does "warrior" mean?

Confront the violence by resisting the violence
Make a credible threat and follow through
Our own people undermine our movements
When it threatens dependency and the chance
To give government hand jobs
Look beyond the petty issues the privilege-laden
Discussions wearing ruts in the path to
Liberation. Get your head together

They are colonizing gender and measuring
Commitment to land with reproduction, reproduction,
reproduction ...
I am tearing up the original instructions
And redefining my tactical needs
I am less interested in the next seven generations
As I am in the now, less a short-sighted vision
And more of a domino strategy
Let 'em roll

Get addicted to the feeling of freedom
A terrorist mindset is the spiritual basis
Found in commitment while we prepare
To articulate a vision to protect what's here
The fasting, the chanting, the grounding
The confronting of our own fear
A warrior's duties are spiritual
Righteous and critical to dismantle
Prison-like constructs

Don't insult me with your consults
Permission will never be granted

The chain of command is changing
Women once a commodity and poster children
For environmental activism are now leading
Stop the poaching of brown skins for
Your causes we are involved in struggles
The likes of which may never be fully understood
Home, where men are pressured to have power
But in the end learn to listen
And we will not roll out our young for the sake
Of your education we will teach them
From here how to be human

Photo courtesy of **Anna Min | Min Enterprises Photography LLC**

Janet Rogers is a Mohawk/Tuscarora writer from the Six Nations band in Ontario. She was born in Vancouver and has been living on the traditional lands of the Coast Salish people in Victoria, British Columbia, since 1994. Janet works in the genres of poetry, spoken-word performance poetry, video poetry, recorded music with poetry, and script writing. From 2012 to 2014, Janet served as Poet Laureate of Victoria.

Janet has published three poetry collections to date: *Splitting the Heart* (Ekstasis Editions, 2007), *Red Erotic* (Ojistah Publishing, 2010), and *Unearthed* (Leaf Press, 2011). Her poetry CDs *Firewater* (2009), *Got Your Back* (2012), and *6 Directions* (2013) all received nominations for Best Spoken Word Recording at the Canadian Aboriginal Music Awards, the Aboriginal Peoples Choice Music Awards, and the Native American Music Awards.

Janet hosts *Native Waves Radio* on CFUV and *Tribal Clefs* on CBC Radio One in Victoria. Her radio documentaries *Bring Your Drum: 50 Years of Indigenous Protest Music* and *Resonating Reconciliation* won Best Radio at the imagineNATIVE Film and Media festival in 2011 and 2013.

Ikkwenyes or Dare to Do is the name of the collective Mohawk poet Alex Jacobs and Janet created in 2011. Ikkwenyes won the Canada Council for the Arts Collaborative Exchange Award in 2012 and a Loft Literary Prize in 2013.

www.janetmarierogers.ca